*Show me the rainbow
you hide under your scars*

Suri Singh

First Edition

The author asserts the moral right under the Copyright, Designs and Patents Act 1988 to be identified as the author of this work.

All Rights reserved. No part of this publication may be reproduced, stored in a retrieval system or transmitted, in any form or by any means without the prior consent of the author, nor be otherwise circulated in any form of binding or cover other than that which it is published and without a similar condition being imposed on the subsequent purchaser.

Copyright © Suri Singh 2022
Book cover by Chloe Henkel

Written and arranged by Suri Singh

About This Book

Over 5 years of dedication has brought the truth to this book. Books become a poetry through your journey of truth. It has shown me the rainbow you hide under your scars which is the collection of poetry and prose adapted into this book about love, relationships, raw emotions and hope.

Every section is dedicated to starting with how you fall in love as it makes life feel magical to how it may fall apart. However, over time your broken life adapts into written poetic truths.

These poems give you the cycle of different life experiences that portray love, obstacles, and faith of journey.

I hope and have faith that this poetic book will work as a balm to your heart.

Suri Singh

I was a broken crown, a king found me, set me on his head and said, "you complete me".

Show me the rainbow you hide under your scars

Honey!
Do you know I have stolen you from bees?

Suri Singh

It's not glow on my face, it's him.

Show me the rainbow you hide under your scars

My skin will wrinkle, my hair will fall, my eyes will see things blurry, my nose will have a hard time to smell, my body will tremble, my back will bend and my voice will fumble, but my heart will beat in the same way for you because, "I Love You".

Suri Singh

We aren't in a relationship yet, but sometimes she fights with me as if I'm her boyfriend and it makes me blush.

Show me the rainbow you hide under your scars

One day the right one will add you to his family group chat on WhatsApp.

Suri Singh

Look at the sky, our stars are aligning tonight.

Show me the rainbow you hide under your scars

Your beauty is not temporary for the permanent one.

First love is like a one-year-old baby, no matter what they do, you will smile.

Show me the rainbow you hide under your scars

Sometimes you hide him in your smile and sometimes you express him in it and you always say you don't have anyone.

Suri Singh

Most people use filters to enhance their beauty, she uses them to hide it, that's how beautiful she is.

Show me the rainbow you hide under your scars

Is it the book "the secret" attracting me towards you?

Suri Singh

We all have someone special officially or unofficially to imagine our life with.

Show me the rainbow you hide under your scars

Dear dream,
Can I see her tonight?

Suri Singh

I think we are getting interested in each other.

Show me the rainbow you hide under your scars

Toma mi mano y llévame a tu mundo.
(Hold my hand and take me to your world)

Suri Singh

How do you know I'm sad?
You don't speak much.
You remove your dp, you deactivate your Instagram.
You delete your snapchat.
And you ignore all friend requests and msgs on Facebook.

Show me the rainbow you hide under your scars

I feel shy when I go out with you, because the entire world looks at us as if we are a newly married couple.

The more I speak to you, the more I reveal my feelings for you.

Show me the rainbow you hide under your scars

Colour my skin with love bites.

Suri Singh

Which fragrance do you love the most?
 "My lovers"

Show me the rainbow you hide under your scars

Your love is divine if she forgets her stomach-ache when you are around.

Suri Singh

Every time I visit a florist, I fail to find a rose more beautiful than her.

Show me the rainbow you hide under your scars

I don't want someone who walks with me and looks at someone else.

Suri Singh

Seeing me naked is what you call love?

Women are like flowers because you smell good too when they are around.

Suri Singh

When I text you "goodnight" it does not always mean I'm going to sleep, sometimes it means talk to me.

Show me the rainbow you hide under your scars

Her make-up kit includes good vibes too.

Suri Singh

It ruins my mood when I wait for you the entire day and awake the whole night and all you say is "I want to sleep".

Show me the rainbow you hide under your scars

Do you know you stay a little longer than usual when you are drunk?

Suri Singh

The right one worries about the weather inside you.

Su cuerpo huele a menta y su amor se siente como marihuana.
(Her body smells like mint and her love feels like marijuana.)

Suri Singh

If she is hiding everything from the world but telling you about it, isn't it something special.

Show me the rainbow you hide under your scars

I wish you said everything to me in person because dream interpretation is not always correct.

Suri Singh

Some days you show me your anger and tell me it's care, it makes me sad but that's okay.

Show me the rainbow you hide under your scars

She turned into ashes but her heart keeps beating for him in someone else's chest.

Suri Singh

In your teens cutting your wrist is love and, in your adulthood, hiding your pain is...

Show me the rainbow you hide under your scars

I want you focused on me the way you are focused on the road while riding a motorbike.

Suri Singh

On last Halloween I was dressed up as a zombie and fell in love with a witch.

Show me the rainbow you hide under your scars

Flirt with her even if she is yours.

Suri Singh

No one can love you more than the one who cried for you.

Show me the rainbow you hide under your scars

How beautiful love is the moment someone falls in love with you. You become a king overnight.

Suri Singh

If you have ever loved in your life, you must have traded your prayers for it too.

Show me the rainbow you hide under your scars

A paper rose smells just like a real rose when you are in love.

Suri Singh

You make me feel like a baby again...
Will you stay the same even after our wedding?

Show me the rainbow you hide under your scars

She knows which colour/style dresses she wants, but she still sends you pictures to help her choose because nothing makes her happier than you choosing a dress she likes.

Suri Singh

You are her special occasion and this is the reason she wears a new dress every time she meets you.

Both of them teach each other something new everyday and then argue over who is the student and who is the teacher, when in reality the pair possesses both traits.

Suri Singh

You are the cure my heart recommends.

Show me the rainbow you hide under your scars

I was just looking at you and you stole my heart.

Suri Singh

Is she white? Black? Brown?
No!
Rainbow.

Show me the rainbow you hide under your scars

I don't hide anything from you, but when you make me sad, I don't tell you.

Suri Singh

She loves herself and this is what makes people jealous.

Show me the rainbow you hide under your scars

No matter how bad you become, your parents will never leave you and that's the kind of love you should be looking for.

Suri Singh

If he likes you, he'll tell his friends.
If he loves you, he'll tell his parents.

Don't doubt the love of those who love you more than their fear of any phobia, like if someone has a fear of water and they jump in it for you or if someone has a fear of heights and they climb mountains for you. Because they never give up on you.

Suri Singh

Do not throw away the fruit when you actually want to throw away its peel.

Show me the rainbow you hide under your scars

When his dead body was examined to determine the cause of his death, his heart tried to pump one more time for her.

Suri Singh

She is the kind of woman that makes everyone believe in love at first sight.

Show me the rainbow you hide under your scars

One day you'll drive your favourite car, with your favourite person to your favourite destination.

Suri Singh

I enjoyed your stay in my life.

Show me the rainbow you hide under your scars

You are breaking my heart and telling me if I cry it will be hard on you. How?

Suri Singh

Sometimes it's hard to know whether you are annoyed or irritated or throwing attitude or just want attention from me.

Show me the rainbow you hide under your scars

I need food for my body to survive and you for my soul too.

Suri Singh

I have not built muscles to look attractive, I have built them to protect you.

Show me the rainbow you hide under your scars

How many times in your relationship did he get on his knees?

Just once is boring though.

I want someone who I can listen to 90s music with.

The phrase "if it's meant to be, we'll be together" does not fit in if you don't want to give your relationship a chance.

Suri Singh

Love does not need motivation, love needs love.

Show me the rainbow you hide under your scars

You would even pick it up from the dirt if it is important to you.

You don't have to work on compatibility, you both have to love each other, that's it.

Show me the rainbow you hide under your scars

Your understanding of each other needs to be more aligned than your stars.

They are not rejecting you, they are rejecting the habits you adopted from your ex.

If they loved you, why did they tell you to convert to their religion? Isn't it a condition?

Suri Singh

I feel drugs and sad songs have no difference, both somehow damage you and make you believe you are enjoying them.

Sometimes you are unable to express your feelings, but they come out through your eyes.

And unfortunately, my mood changes with your behaviour.

Show me the rainbow you hide under your scars

Why do you put so much make up on?
"To hide his sins".

Suri Singh

Feelings do not have errors.

Show me the rainbow you hide under your scars

Why didn't you speak to her today?
At 23:59 my heart whispered.

You can unsend all your texts but not your feelings attached to them.

Taking a break from each other should not mean giving space to someone else.

Suri Singh

I don't want a relationship in which you have to turn your internet off to hide someone else's frequent texts while meeting me.

Show me the rainbow you hide under your scars

Your words last night did not let our relationship wake up this morning.

The most painful truth is I loved you, and the most beautiful lie is you loved me too.

Show me the rainbow you hide under your scars

Let's not talk if your intention is to break my heart.

I don't miss you but I terribly miss the one in you who once truly loved me.

Show me the rainbow you hide under your scars

I just have you in my circle.

Suri Singh

Are you missing me or using me to forget someone?

Show me the rainbow you hide under your scars

Everyone on this planet is sensitive about something or someone.

Suri Singh

How loyal were you to him?
I did not even know how it feels like to talk to another man.

Show me the rainbow you hide under your scars

This generation might choose 3 am to break your heart.

Suri Singh

I still possess our old texts/pictures together but I can't look at them when I'm sober because it is like examining a dead body and finding out the reason of its death.

Spending time alone, turning all lights off, listening to sad songs and wiping your tears off.

Don't you think this has become a kind of addiction?

Suri Singh

You are damn lucky because you live with the one, I have memories with.

Show me the rainbow you hide under your scars

How can they be your best friend if they don't know you love them?

You said everything was okay... and now you are breaking up.

Show me the rainbow you hide under your scars

Maybe you are linking the right song with the wrong person.

Are you losing interest in me or getting interested in someone else?

Show me the rainbow you hide under your scars

We were too young when we broke up.

Suri Singh

Tu amor era un cubito de hielo, que se derritió con tus mentiras
(Your love was an ice cube, that melted with your lies.)

Show me the rainbow you hide under your scars

You are not lost it is just their world does not make sense to you.

If we were dating, I would arrange-rearrange your room every time I visit you.

Dear Ex,
Does your mother-in-law love you as much as my mother did?

Suri Singh

How can everything be normal again when I'm married to someone else, and you are to someone else.

How easy it has become to meet anyone, anytime, anywhere in the world and how complicated it is to stay with just one.

Suri Singh

You stayed longer in my bed than my life.

Show me the rainbow you hide under your scars

The world isn't silent, your pain is too loud.

Imagine you are thinking about your future with someone and at the same time they text you saying "don't rely on me for anything".

Show me the rainbow you hide under your scars

Aren't tears answer sometimes?

Suri Singh

Stop counting how long it would've been if you were still together.

Show me the rainbow you hide under your scars

When you are telling something to someone and it makes your voice shaky, your heart heavy and you end up crying, that's real pain.

Suri Singh

I don't want you to change, I want you to leave.

Show me the rainbow you hide under your scars

I don't want to ask you anything because the long gaps between my texts and yours answers all my questions.

Suri Singh

Did you sleep peacefully last night?
Then what makes you think they love you?

Show me the rainbow you hide under your scars

They have time for you until you surrender your body.

Suri Singh

They say the world would end one day but mine has ended the day you left me.

Show me the rainbow you hide under your scars

My mom said, "don't marry someone who is with you on paper and physically with someone else."

Suri Singh

Except your heart.
I admire everything in black.

Show me the rainbow you hide under your scars

I'm not a demon, it is just you killed the angel in me.

If we ever meet again, would you be able to look at me with your chin up?

Show me the rainbow you hide under your scars

It hurts when you call my beautiful moment with you "regrets".

Suri Singh

Are these dark circles under your eyes or the stories you don't want to talk about?

Show me the rainbow you hide under your scars

When they lie to you, they start contradicting themselves.

Suri Singh

Harming yourself won't bring them back.

The song you are listening to on repeat, is it to comfort yourself or to make yourself cry?

Suri Singh

They make fun of me because you were not loyal.

Show me the rainbow you hide under your scars

I read our story again and again except the page on which you replaced me.

If I had been able to visit my past, I would bring you to my present. That's how much I loved you.

Every day when I see birds going back home, it gives me hope that one day you'll come back too.

In every person's life there are some memories, maybe unwanted, which one wants to put them in a trunk, lock them up and throw in the ocean.

Show me the rainbow you hide under your scars

How many times did you feel like not getting off the train when you reach your destination?

Virginity is not an issue anymore, trust is.

Show me the rainbow you hide under your scars

If they lie to their parents for you, they will surely lie to you one day for someone else.

Suri Singh

Your true friends know the one you can't forget.

Show me the rainbow you hide under your scars

Scan the entire world, I would not be found in anyone.

Suri Singh

You won't understand my feelings because you have to have a heart.

You were the closest person I ever had. Now who to tell that you broke my heart?

Suri Singh

When someone dies you can't keep their body, can you? Similarly, do not expect them to keep you in their life when their love for you dies. Move on.

Someday, somewhere, something will remind you of me.

And slowly-slowly everything ended between us.

Show me the rainbow you hide under your scars

Possessing a clean heart costs too much.

If the end result comes out to be true, you were not doubting them, you already knew they were cheating on you.

You've left memories too, someday they will make them cry too.

Suri Singh

When we kissed only you knew it was our last one.

Show me the rainbow you hide under your scars

You can't lift much when your hand/leg is broken and you understand this too, but you carry too much when your heart is broken and you don't understand it.

Suri Singh

How was your youth?
Sad.

Don't talk about my looks, it has never attracted someone loyal.

Suri Singh

Once in a blue moon everyone reads the unclosed chapter of their life with filled eyes.

Begging them is like making them eat something they don't like anymore, and even if you succeed eventually, they'll puke everything out.

Suri Singh

Your lie saves you but hurts me.

The one who teaches you how to love never tells you how to heal.

Your sleeping pattern, eating disorder, and weight gain will get back to normal when you start focusing on yourself again.

Silence could mean yes, no, not interested or you don't deserve an answer.

Maybe you looked at the right thing but you picked something else.

Show me the rainbow you hide under your scars

Not everyone knows how to hold something beautiful.

Sometimes music makes you relive an old memory.

Maybe their prayers are much more powerful for you than your bad intentions for yourself.

Are you not happy with your life or the people in it?
You can change both.

"I don't want to give everything to someone before marriage" I hope you understand what I mean.
But you know when you are in love you just go with the flow... don't you?

En ocasiones no puedes ni enfrentarte al sol pero eso no significa que estes mal
(Sometimes you can't even face the sun but that does not mean you are wrong.)

Show me the rainbow you hide under your scars

We are not here to spend some years with someone and then switch to another person to find something new.

Make some mistakes, your future self needs them.

My dad once said, "if you be as stubborn as you were in your childhood, you can get anything you want in the world."

Your beauty can make them strike up a conversation but your brain can make them stay.

Show me the rainbow you hide under your scars

Your condition, your situation and your emotions never lie.

Suri Singh

Sometimes roads are empty but there is too much traffic in your head.

Show me the rainbow you hide under your scars

When the dark phase gets longer, we all get addicted to something.

Suri Singh

You are safe in your own hands.

Show me the rainbow you hide under your scars

It should not take your entire youth to say what you feel.

Suri Singh

I know how to dress up, how to cook and how to live alone.

Do not let someone down who has invested kindness in you.

Suri Singh

Even at an unknown station, you'll find your way to the exit.

Show me the rainbow you hide under your scars

Have you ever seen seven colours in the sky?
You are more than that.

Suri Singh

Sometimes at night I don't want a dessert, I want new books.

Do not criticise your appearance there must be someone who prays everyday to find a woman like you.

Doubting your abilities is like testing the light in the light and dark in the dark.

Show me the rainbow you hide under your scars

You are not old, you've just forgotten how to live a life.

If inspiration does not get converted into actions, you are not inspired yet.

Don't measure your success by who you portray as not successful.

Do not destroy your perfect life in search of a perfect life.

Show me the rainbow you hide under your scars

The girl you left drowning has become a mermaid.

Fresh air brings dirt too.

Show me the rainbow you hide under your scars

When you start liking yourself you won't need to choose the best picture out of the five you have clicked to show to the world, you would pick all of them.

Everything you repeat is either pleasure, pain or a mistake.

Show me the rainbow you hide under your scars

Beautiful were the days when a crowned pencil, a heart-shaped sharpener, a rose fragranced rubber and a square geometry box seemed like the biggest treasure in the world.

If you ask them something and they say "it's a personal question", you are not true friends yet.

Show me the rainbow you hide under your scars

If you keep checking the time, you are not enjoying the process of whatever you are doing.

Using negative words damages you too.

Show me the rainbow you hide under your scars

If you are making something out of greed don't call it art.

If you all come together as a family no one will drown ever. Whether it is something mentally, physically or financially, like if you have watched the end of Titanic wherein all small boats come together and make more space in order to save more lives.

Show me the rainbow you hide under your scars

If someone has tried something and has failed, it does not mean you'll fail too.

Suri Singh

One day kindness will find you.

Show me the rainbow you hide under your scars

Maybe in old age you'll realise you were beautiful when you were young.

If you are leaving yourself too, there is no difference between you and them.

Do not compare your one sad day with someone's highlights of the year.

Suri Singh

When you die and go up somewhere in the sky.
Will you say, "I'm from America or Europe or Asia."
Or "I'm brown or white or black"? You won't because we are one human race.

Show me the rainbow you hide under your scars

Thinking about the good old days makes me believe that life can be beautiful again.

Suri Singh

Do not sell your sunny days.

Spending time thinking about your old days isn't always a bad use of time.

The truth is people only make quick changes to how they appear.

Unfortunately, we teach our daughters how to do the dishes instead of how to fight.

Suri Singh

Do not overthink about your future, you might not even exist.

Show me the rainbow you hide under your scars

Richness is not always what you see in your bank account, it is what you have on your face.

It's saddening that the ones who survive die too.

Show me the rainbow you hide under your scars

A kind heart never fills anyone's head with hatred.

Suri Singh

When someone commits a mistake, you correct them you don't abuse them.

Show me the rainbow you hide under your scars

If someone has left you, you need help not their replacement.

Less followers on social media does not mean you are incapable.

If you recall a moment and it makes you laugh you've really lived that moment.

Suri Singh

When someone dies, their version of you dies too.

Isn't it tough to respond to questions like "why haven't you slept yet?"

Suri Singh

If life was long, it would not fit in a 3-hour movie.

Show me the rainbow you hide under your scars

Sometimes standing near the window makes you feel light.

Suri Singh

If you are late somewhere or to someone or to something it does not mean you are useless. Know your worth.

Show me the rainbow you hide under your scars

A wallet full of money gives you confidence.

Suri Singh

You don't let them spend your money but you let them waste your time, how funny it is.

Show me the rainbow you hide under your scars

I didn't give up because I had a burning desire to see the bloody brilliant version of myself.

Suri Singh

The door you are knocking at has nothing to offer except a wall.

Show me the rainbow you hide under your scars

I'm happy and that's my strength.

No matter how expensive your dreams are never stop dreaming.

Have you seen a tree with no leaves on? This is how you look when you don't smile.

Suri Singh

You can't spend "today" better in the future.

Show me the rainbow you hide under your scars

The good thing about being alone is you start recognizing yourself.

Do not try to translate everything in your own language, you might misinterpret or change the actual meaning.

The world might give up on you, but the universe will not because you are its own creation.

Suri Singh

If you have not seen them doing something good for the world, it does not mean they are bad people.

Show me the rainbow you hide under your scars

Sometimes newly painted walls have dirty stories.

About The Author

Suri Singh is an author, content creator and a self-taught programmer. He lives in the United Kingdom.

He developed a passion for writing while being inspired after exploring historical landmarks.

Apart from writing, he loves to travel and explore new places. He loves sharing photos of his favourite places to eat, lifestyle and books on both these Instagram pages, @thiscrazygeneration and @surisingh_writer.

Suri is a self-help coach, providing invaluable advice to those who are experiencing difficulties in their personal relationships, both romantic and non-romantic. For Suri, giving people hope during their journey, and being the reason they smile is the most fulfilling job he could do.

www.ingramcontent.com/pod-product-compliance
Lightning Source LLC
Chambersburg PA
CBHW020904080526
44589CB00011B/440